# MONSTER Airplanes

by Chris Bowman

AIRFRANCE
JD

BLASTOFF! READERS 1

BELLWETHER MEDIA • MINNEAPOLIS, MN

Note to Librarians, Teachers, and Parents:

**Blastoff! Readers** are carefully developed by literacy experts and combine standards-based content with developmentally appropriate text.

**Level 1** provides the most support through repetition of high-frequency words, light text, predictable sentence patterns, and strong visual support.

**Level 2** offers early readers a bit more challenge through varied simple sentences, increased text load, and less repetition of high-frequency words.

**Level 3** advances early-fluent readers toward fluency through increased text and concept load, less reliance on visuals, longer sentences, and more literary language.

**Level 4** builds reading stamina by providing more text per page, increased use of punctuation, greater variation in sentence patterns, and increasingly challenging vocabulary.

**Level 5** encourages children to move from "learning to read" to "reading to learn" by providing even more text, varied writing styles, and less familiar topics.

Whichever book is right for your reader, Blastoff! Readers are the perfect books to build confidence and encourage a love of reading that will last a lifetime!

This edition first published in 2014 by Bellwether Media, Inc.



Library of Congress Cataloging-in-Publication Data

Bowman, Chris, 1990-
Monster Airplanes / by Chris Bowman.
pages cm – (Blastoff! Readers. Monster Machines)
Includes bibliographical references and index.
Summary: "Developed by literacy experts for students in kindergarten through grade three, this book introduces airplanes to young readers through leveled text and related photos"–Provided by publisher.
Audience: K-3.
ISBN 978-1-62617-052-0 (hardcovers : alk. paper)
1. Airplanes–Juvenile literature. I. Title.
TL547.B6788 2014
387.7'334–dc23

2013035103



Printed in the United States of America, North Mankato, MN.

# Table of Contents

# Jumbo Jets!

Jumbo jets carry people to places far away. These airplanes fly fast and up high.

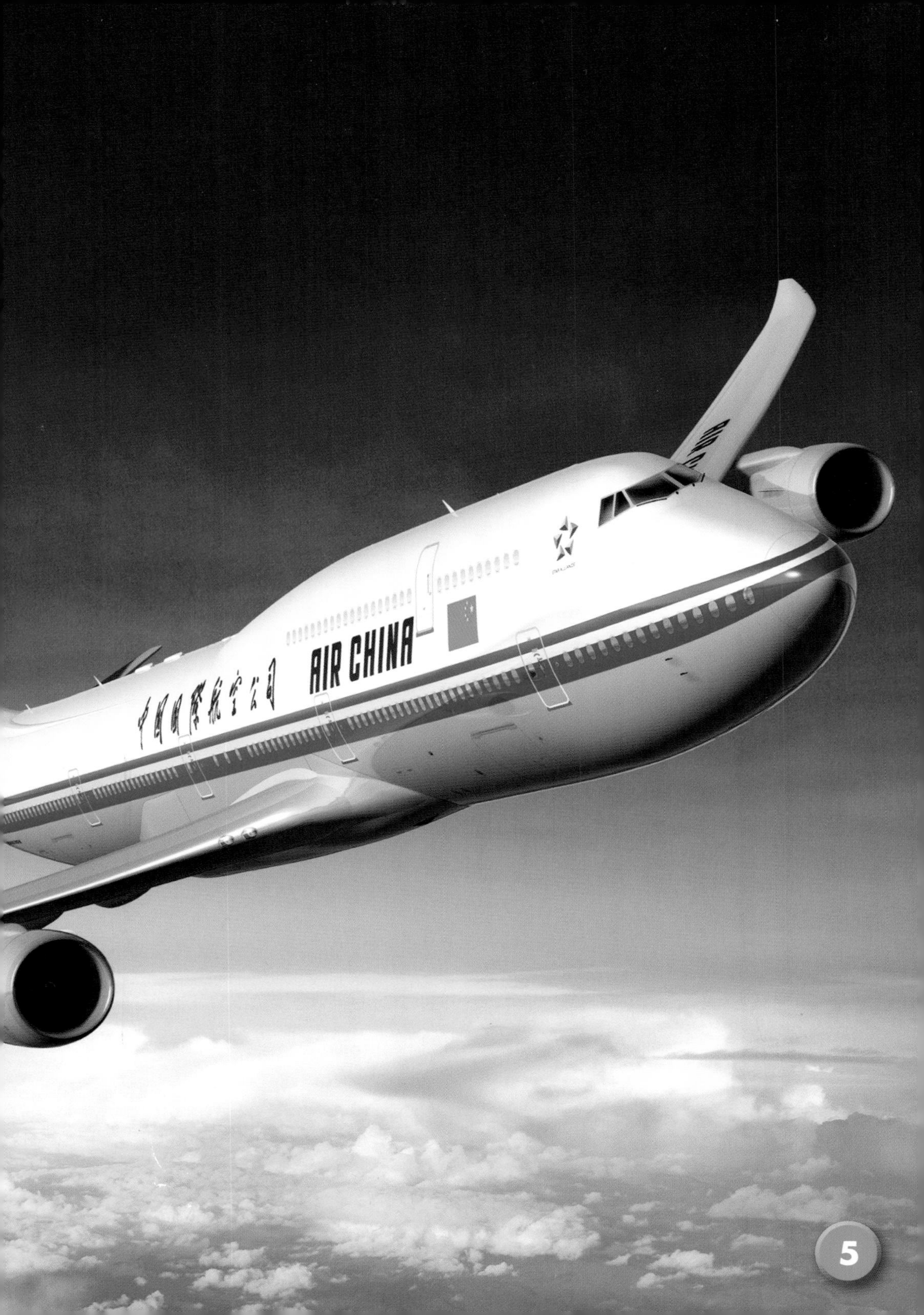
中國國際航空公司
AIR CHINA

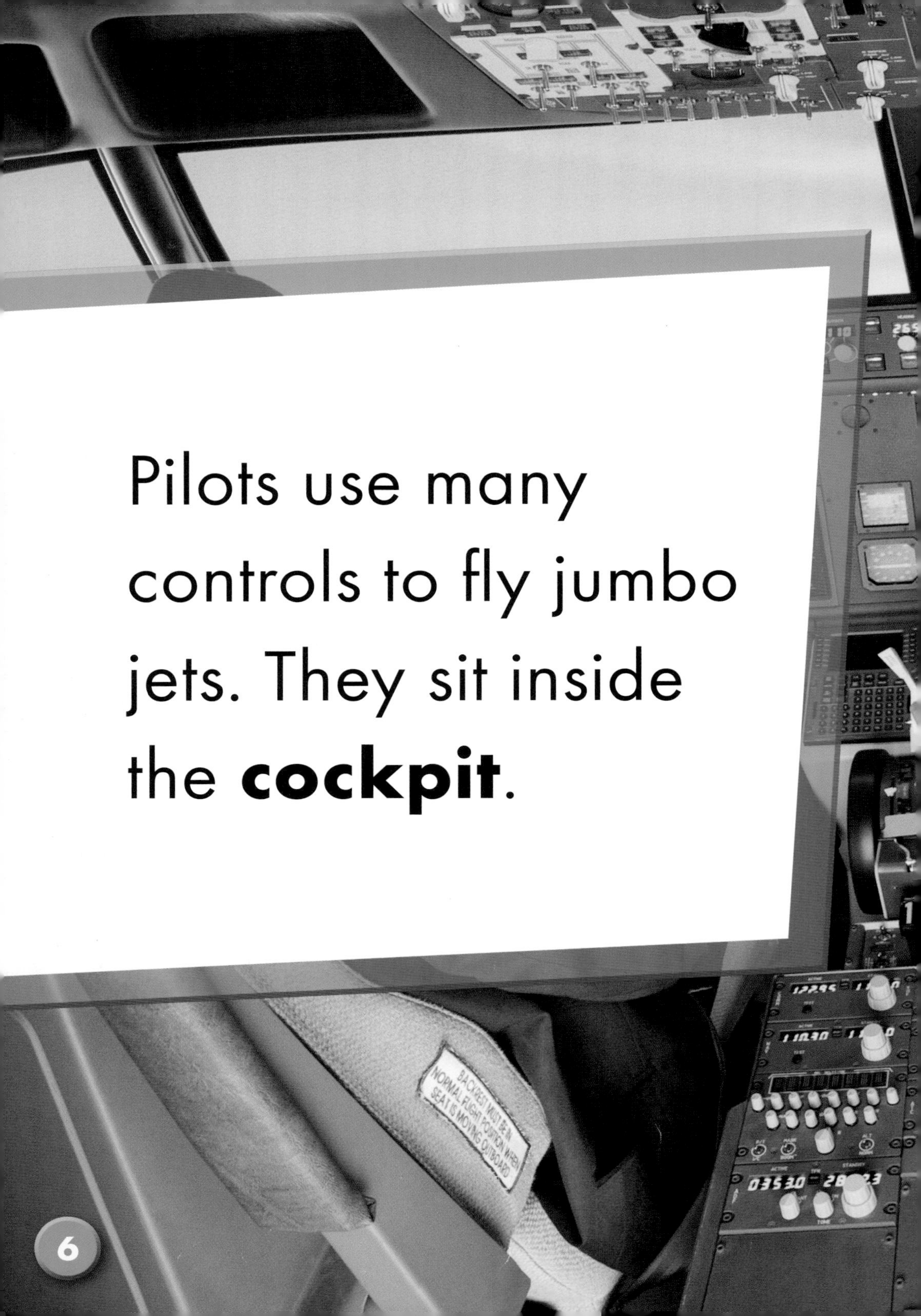
BACKREST MUST BE IN
NORMAL FLIGHT POSITION WHEN
SEAT IS MOVING OUTBOARD

Pilots use many controls to fly jumbo jets. They sit inside the **cockpit**.

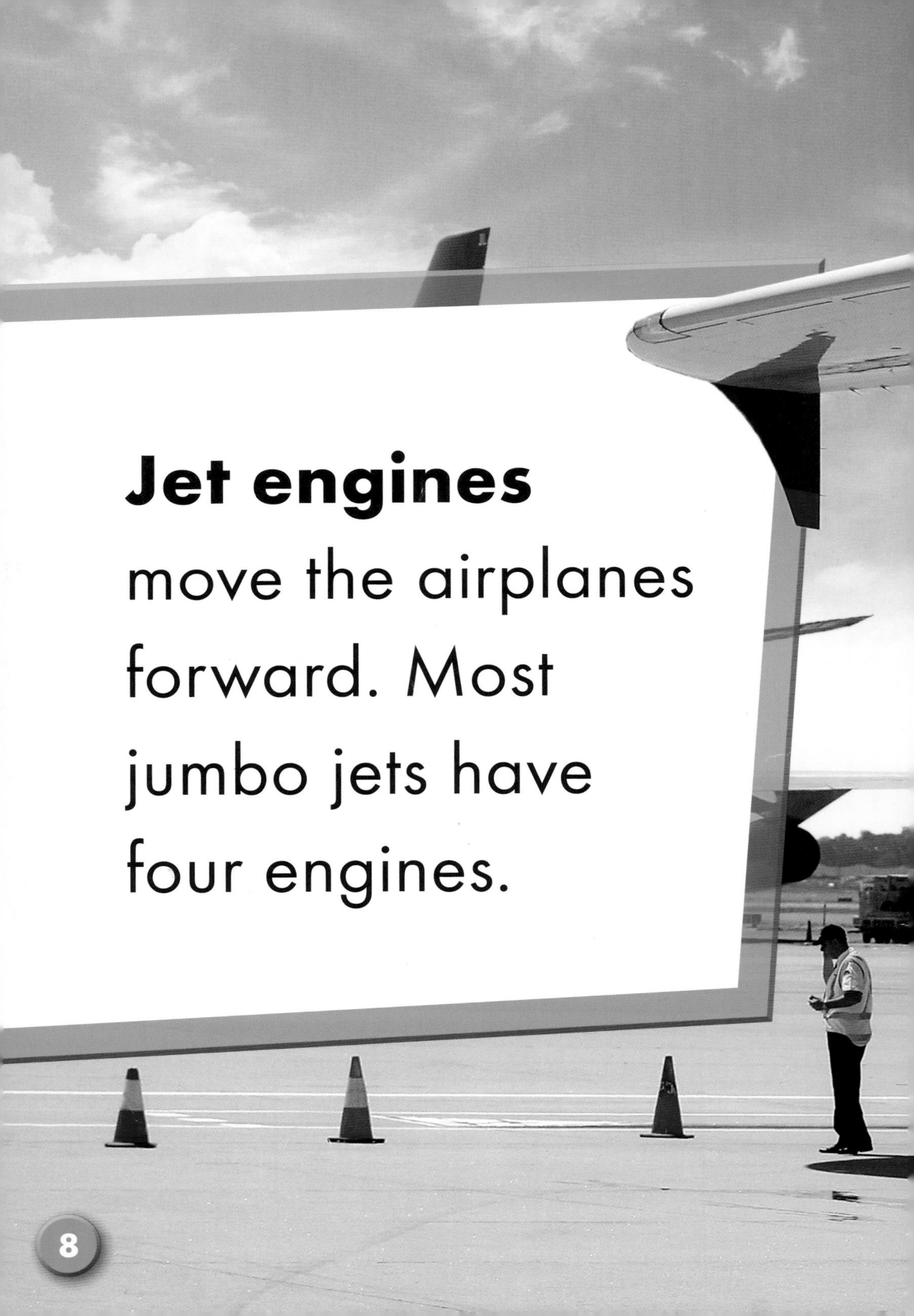

**Jet engines** move the airplanes forward. Most jumbo jets have four engines.

jet engine

Some jumbo jets are **double-deckers**. They have two levels of seats.

The largest jets have seats for more than 800 people!

ice

ANA

# Cargo Planes

Huge **cargo** planes do not carry people. They fly heavy loads from place to place.

Some cargo planes bring supplies to **military zones**.

Other cargo planes give **space shuttles** a ride!

Endeavour
HE 40

# Monster Hangars

Jumbo jets and cargo planes park in giant **hangars**. They hang out here between flights!

hangar

# Glossary

**cargo**—goods that are carried by an airplane, ship, or truck

**cockpit**—the front part of an airplane where the pilot sits

**double-deckers**—airplanes or other vehicles that have two floors of seats

**hangars**—big buildings that hold airplanes

**jet engines**—machines that power jet airplanes

**military zones**—areas where soldiers fight

**space shuttles**—aircraft that carry people and cargo in space

# To Learn More

## AT THE LIBRARY

Ohmann, Paul R. *How Airplanes Work.* Mankato, Minn.: Child's World, 2012.

Schaefer, Lola M. *Airplanes in Action.* Mankato, Minn.: Capstone Press, 2012.

Wiseman, Blaine. *Jumbo Jets.* New York, N.Y.: Weigl Publishers, 2011.

## ON THE WEB

Learning more about airplanes is as easy as 1, 2, 3.

1. Go to www.factsurfer.com.
2. Enter "airplanes" into the search box.
3. Click the "Surf" button and you will see a list of related Web sites.

With factsurfer.com, finding more information is just a click away.

# Index




The images in this book are reproduced through the courtesy of: Daniel Zuckerkandel, front cover; Boeing Corporation, pp. 4-5; Westend61/ SuperStock, pp. 6-7; Greg Wood/ Getty Images, pp. 8-9; Pavel L Photo and Video, pp. 10-11; Philippe Turpin/ Glow Images, pp. 12-13; Paul Fell, pp. 14-15; Department of Defense/ Air Force, pp. 16-17; Associated Press, pp. 18-19; Christian Charisius/ Reuters/ Newscom, pp. 20-21.